Penguin, Penguin

For the earliest reader

by Margaret Hillert

Starfall™
www.starfall.com

Other Starfall Books
by Margaret Hillert

Happy Mother's Day, Dear Dragon
Not Too Little to Help
The No-Tail Cat
Three Little Plays

This book is part of the
"I'm Reading!" fluent reading sequence
featured on

www.**starfall**.com

This series is designed to encourage reading
fluency. It allows children to achieve mastery
and confidence by reading substantial books
(both fiction and non-fiction) that use a
limited vocabulary of sight words. "Step 1"
refers to the easiest group of books in this series.
It can be read after, or at the same time as,
Starfall's well-known Learn-to-Read phonics
series featuring Zac the Rat™ and other tales.

Text copyright © 2004 by Margaret Hillert.
Graphics © 2004 Starfall Publications. All rights reserved.
Photo on page 24 by Ann Barker. Used by permission.
Starfall is a registered trademark with the U.S. Patent and Trademark
Office. The content of this book is protected by the laws of copyright
and trademark in the U.S.A. and other countries. Printed in China.

ISBN: 1-59577-020-8

Starfall Publications
P.O. Box 359, Boulder, Colorado 80306

Oh, oh, oh.
Look here. Look here.
What will you find here?

Here is something.
How big it is!
Big, big, big.

And look at this one.

See the spots on it.

This is a pretty one.

This one is pretty, too.
Look at it go.
It can go up, up, up.

Now look here.
What is this?
How funny!

Here is a father.
And here is a mother.
The father and the mother
make something.

What is this?
What will the mother do
with this?
Will she sit on it?

No, no.

She will not sit on it.

She will go away to eat.

Away, away, away.

Here is the father.
Look at the father.
See what he will do.

This is work for the father.
Work, work, work.
But he wants to do it.

Oh, look now.
A little baby.
A little, little baby.

Here comes the mother.
Now the father can go.
The mother will look out
for the baby.

The baby wants to eat.
See what the mother can do.
This is how the baby eats.
What a funny way to eat!

The baby can play, too.
It likes to play.
All the babies like to play.

Something big is here.
Look at this big one.
It wants something to eat.
Will it get the baby?

No, no.

See the mother run at it.

It will not get the baby.

The mother looks out for
the baby.

Now look at the baby.
See how big it is!
Big, big, big.

The mother and father
will go away now.
Away, away, away.
What will the baby do?

See the baby run.

Run, run, run.

He is black and white now.

He looks like the mother
and father.

He is big now.
He will go away, too.
He will go to look for
something to eat.

More Information about Penguins

Penguin, Penguin is about the Adelie penguin. The Adelie penguin makes its home on Antarctica, near the South Pole.

Not all penguins live in cold places. Penguins also live in New Zealand, Argentina, Chile, Peru, South Africa, the Falkland Islands, and the Galapagos Islands, near the equator. There are 17 different species of penguins in the world.

Penguins do not live in the Arctic, near the North Pole.

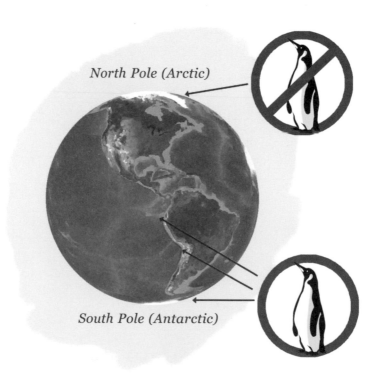

North Pole (Arctic)

South Pole (Antarctic)

Here are pictures of some other kinds of penguins.

Erect-Crested Penguin

Chinstrap Penguin

Emperor Penguin

Gentoo Penguin

About the Author

Margaret Hillert wrote her first poem when she was eight years old. At eighty-five she's still writing books and poems for children and adults all around the world.

Margaret knows what children like to read because she was a first-grade teacher for 34 years. She loves to visit her local library and read to children.

The Women's National Book Association honored Margaret in 1993 for writing wonderful children's books. But she says her BIGGEST reward has been teaching so many children how to read!

Vocabulary - 58 Words

a	he	see
all	here	she
and	how	sit
at	is	something
away	it	spots
babies	likes	the
baby	little	this
big	look(s)	to
black	make	too
but	mother	up
can	no	wants
comes	not	way
do	now	what
eat(s)	oh	white
father	on	will
find	one	with
for	out	work
funny	play	you
get	pretty	
go	run	